To:

From:

Happy Together

500 Things to Do for and with Your Sweetheart

KEN SHAFER
ILLUSTRATED BY TOM SZAFRANSKI

CONTEMPORARY BOOKS
A TRIBUNE COMPANY

Shafer, Ken.
    Happy together : 500 things to do for and with your sweetheart/
Ken Shafer; illustrated by Tom Szafranski.

        p.   cm
    ISBN 0-8092-3154-9
    1. Man-woman relationships.   2. Love.   3. Intimacy (Psychology)
    1. Title.
    HQ801.S466   1996
    646.7'8—dc20   96-7503
                                                         CIP

Illustrations by Tom Szafranski

Published by Contemporary Books, Inc.
Two Prudential Plaza, Chicago, Illinois 60601-6790
Manufactured in the United States of America
International Standard Book Number: 0-8092-3154-9
10 9 8 7 6 5 4 3 2 1

To Sherry

Preface

The impetus for writing *Happy Together* was my lifestyle with someone very close to me. Sherry and I started dating on Christmas Day, 1988. Since then, she and I have done a tremendous number of things for and with each other.

As our anniversaries approached, people remarked how seldom nonmarried couples stay together for as long as we have. Many people asked what our secret is, but there really is none. We have simply been happy together.

It became apparent to me that many couples could use a guide for structuring their relationships. I thought that listing what she and I have done over the years could help to provide stability and amusement for them.

Presented here are 500 concise and active ideas for enhancing, improving, and saving a relationship. Most of them are from personal experience, and this list is certainly not complete. I hope this book gives insight about the kind of happiness Sherry and I still experience every day.

Acknowledgments

God, Mom, Dad, Jeanne, the United States of America, Mike and Dobias, Jerrold Jenkins, Tom Szafranski, my relatives, Benji, Sandy, C.L., Benji II, B.L., Treen, J.R., Richard Nixon—thanks for your autograph—rest in peace, the 1980s, HOJO Room 515, London Tower Bridge ("Oh, Ken—look!"—Sherry), the late-night talk shows during which I wrote this book, Traverse City, Michigan—home of the National Cherry Festival, Jennifer Nelson, literary agent Rebecca Austin for talking me into it, and, last but not least, my not-yet-born children.

1. Be yourself with your sweetheart.

2. Be honest with your sweetheart.

3. Wear the same kind of sweatshirts.

4. Have faith that the two of you will always be together.

5. Mention to your sweetheart how great he looks.

6. Tell your sweetheart a joke.

7. Call in sick together.

8. Take a helicopter ride with your sweetheart.

9. Light fireworks together.

10. Use the numbers of your sweetheart's birthday as your lottery numbers.

11. Get your wedding bands cleaned together.

12. Buy your sweetheart a bottle of her favorite perfume.

13. Offer to be the designated driver when you and your sweetheart go out.

14. Buy your sweetheart a stuffed animal.

15. Go on a hayride together.

16. Go fishing together.

17. Save up enough money for you and your sweetheart to go to Disney World.

18. Give each other a back rub.

19. Buy your sweetheart a magazine.

20. Openly recognize the fact that your sweetheart is intelligent.

21. Sunbathe together.

22. Tell your sweetheart you'd marry him all over again.

23. President Harry Truman mailed his wife a letter every night he spent away; do the same for your sweetheart.

24. Pinch your sweetheart's butt.

25. Watch planes take off and land together.

26. Pray together.

27. Tell your sweetheart about a dream you had.

28. Have flowers sent to your sweetheart at work.

29. Celebrate your anniversary monthly.

30. Play a board game together.

31. Make sure your sweetheart's car is well maintained.

32. Look through an antique store together.

33. Buy your sweetheart a king-sized pillow.

34. Write to your sweetheart's favorite celebrity for an autographed photo.

35. Play frisbee together.

36. Smile at your sweetheart.

37. Look in old newspapers to find out what was happening on the day the two of you met.

38. Buy your sweetheart a dress for a future date.

39. Go snowmobiling together.

40. Give your sweetheart a foot massage.

41. Draw a picture for your sweetheart.

42. Visit your sweetheart's parents.

43. Carve your names in a tree.

44. Tell your sweetheart how lucky you are that she is with you.

45. Ask your sweetheart how her friends are doing.

46. Drop your sweetheart off at a store's entrance and park the car by yourself.

47. Fill a videotape with episodes of your sweetheart's favorite TV show.

48. Go out for dessert together.

49. Have a picture taken with your sweetheart in a photo booth.

50. Give credit to your sweetheart for supporting you when you achieve something.

51. Wear matching outfits.

52. Write your sweetheart a poem.

53. Leave a rose on your sweetheart's pillow.

54. Fax a note to your sweetheart at work.

55. Paint watercolors together.

56. Take a drive through the country together.

57. Tell your sweetheart that he is better-looking than the day the two of you met.

58. Surprise your sweetheart with a candlelight dinner.

59. Tell your sweetheart that meeting him was the main event of your life.

60. Keep your sweetheart's picture in your wallet.

61. Enter a drawing for a prize together.

62. Go bird-watching together.

63. Take part in your sweetheart's aspirations.

64. Do some of your sweetheart's usual chores.

65. Offer to help your sweetheart study.

66. Watch the sunset or sunrise together.

67. Say "I love you" to your sweetheart at least once a day.

68. Play a video game together.

69. Tell your sweetheart she has a perfect face.

70. Make your sweetheart a big lunch.

71. Have a good sense of humor when your sweetheart teases you.

72. Make a home movie together.

73. Hold hands with your sweetheart.

74. Stay up all night watching a movie trilogy together.

75. Follow your sweetheart's family traditions.

76. Go Christmas shopping together.

77. Buy your sweetheart a treat when you pay for gasoline.

78. Take your sweetheart to his favorite restaurant.

79. Tell your sweetheart that she means more to you than anything in the world.

80. Touch your sweetheart as often as possible.

81. Go golfing together.

82. Go out for pizza together.

83. Look at stars together.

84. Throw a boomerang together.

85. Secretly work a second job and use the extra money to surprise your sweetheart with a special gift.

86. Have a professional photo taken of you with your sweetheart.

87. Draw up coupons redeemable for whatever your sweetheart likes.

88. Go out for doughnuts together.

89. Put in a front porch swing.

90. Go white-water rafting together.

91. Buy your sweetheart a favorite
compact disc.

92. Climb a mountain together.

93. Go horseback riding together.

94. Make a list of baby names together.

95. Wear the brand of cologne your sweetheart likes.

96. Build each other a snowman.

97. Plan out quality time for you and your sweetheart.

98. Take a road trip together.

99. Be with your sweetheart when she gives birth.

100. Volunteer for a charity together.

101. Make love on your lunch hour.

102. Tell your sweetheart that she is your best friend.

103. Go to Sunday brunch together.

104. Shop for furniture together.

105. Say something your sweetheart would like to hear.

106. After a fight, make up before going to sleep.

107. Organize your sweetheart's closet.

108. Sing to your sweetheart.

109. Go to church together.

110. Fill up your sweetheart's gas tank.

111. Go to a play together.

112. Watch fireworks together.

113. Leave your sweetheart a message
on his answering machine.

114. Offer to let your sweetheart have her choice of seat on an airplane.

115. Go to a concert together.

116. Make a family tree.

117. Renew your wedding vows.

118. Get tickets for you and your sweetheart to a taping of a TV show you both like.

119. Explore a cave together.

120. Join a club together.

121. Start traditions for you and your sweetheart.

122. Read each other a story.

123. Shop for bargains together.

124. Make a list of predictions together.

125. Tell your sweetheart something that will make him feel important.

126. Go bowling together.

127. Pick berries together.

128. Write a letter to your unborn child together.

129. Visit your sweetheart at work.

130. Spontaneously call your sweetheart to say "I love you."

131. Draw your sweetheart a cartoon.

132. Take a hike together.

133. Prolong the gift-opening experience for your sweetheart. Instead of giving one gift, give many individually wrapped gifts.

134. Take a mud bath together.

135. Announce your milestone
anniversary in the newspaper.

136. Buy your sweetheart a remote
control compatible with the TV,
VCR, and stereo.

137. Play tennis together.

138. Go to a carnival together.

139. Ask your sweetheart how his day went.

140. Offer to buy your sweetheart a drink.

141. Have the poster of your sweetheart's favorite movie framed for her.

142. Make breakfast in bed for your sweetheart.

143. Brag about your sweetheart.

144. Rent a limousine together.

145. Keep a photo album of you with your sweetheart.

146. Buy your sweetheart a book.

147. Join a softball team together.

148. Go jogging together.

149. Save the letters your sweetheart gives you.

150. Take skydiving lessons together.

151. Rent the video of the first movie you saw with your sweetheart and watch it again.

152. Surprise your sweetheart with the best champagne you can afford.

153. Watch sports together.

154. Go out for coffee together.

155. Give your sweetheart a pedicure.

156. Visit a foreign country together.

157. Start an aquarium together.

158. Let your sweetheart spend time with his friends.

159. Make a list of plans for the future.

160. Ask your sweetheart's friends and family for gift ideas.

161. Barbecue together.

162. Make a tape of your sweetheart's favorite music.

163. Rent a paddleboat together.

164. Go to the zoo together.

165. Watch a lightning storm together.

166. Be extra nice to your sweetheart when she has PMS.

167. If you support different candidates, bet dinner and a movie on who wins the election.

168. Get ice cream together.

169. Make up a nickname for your sweetheart.

170. Cook your sweetheart's favorite meal.

171. Insure your wedding rings.

172. If you make more money than your sweetheart, spend some of that extra money on the two of you.

173. Throw your sweetheart a surprise birthday party.

174. Hide a gift in a place where your sweetheart will eventually stumble upon it.

175. Cuddle with your sweetheart every day.

176. Wash your sweetheart's hair.

177. When your sweetheart misses a favorite TV show, tape it

If I have to study

178. Go skinny-dipping together.

179. Have a picnic lunch together.

180. Make your sweetheart a sandwich and cut it in the shape of a heart.

181. Tell people how you met your sweetheart.

182. Have your hair cut the way your sweetheart likes it.

183. Walk on the beach together.

184. Take a martial arts class together.

185. Say "bless you" when your sweetheart sneezes.

186. Get your sweetheart a personalized bathrobe.

187. Go to the highest point in the city at night and look at the lights together.

Any Town
U.S.A.

188. Take an ocean cruise together.

189. Buy your sweetheart a basket of fruit.

190. Have a calendar made with photos of you and your sweetheart.

191. Do the laundry together.

192. Make a pact not to fight in front of anyone—especially the kids.

193. Play footsie with your sweetheart.

194. Brush your sweetheart's hair.

195. Watch home movies together.

196. Learn how to play a musical instrument together.

197. Let the answering machine take your phone calls when you're spending time together.

198. Make pottery together.

199. Forgive your sweetheart for past mistakes.

200. Go parasailing together.

201. Buy your sweetheart an assortment of imported beers.

202. Keep a large picture of your sweetheart in your office.

203. Learn magic tricks and perform them for your sweetheart.

204. Meet on your lunch hours.

205. Go to garage sales together.

206. Go scuba diving together.

207. Keep your anniversary and your sweetheart's birthday marked on your calendar.

208. Share the bathroom.

209. Start a business together.

210. Keep a consistent dinnertime for you and your sweetheart.

211. Make your sweetheart a card.

212. Buy your sweetheart a new pair of slippers.

213. Take a nap together.

214. Visit sick people in the hospital together.

215. Go to a pancake breakfast together.

216. Get tattoos of each other's names.

217. Attend a weight-loss program together.

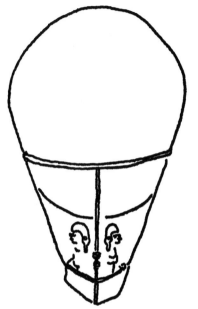

218. Go for a ride
in a hot air balloon together.

219. Go bike riding together.

220. Build a fire for you and your sweetheart.

221. Throw a family reunion.

222. Start a garden together.

223. Bring your sweetheart something from a bakery.

224. Shoot targets together.

225. Get married.

226. Go window shopping together.

227. Snow ski together.

228. Kiss your sweetheart when the clock strikes midnight on New Year's Eve.

22Ỹ. Lend your sweetheart as much
money as she wants.

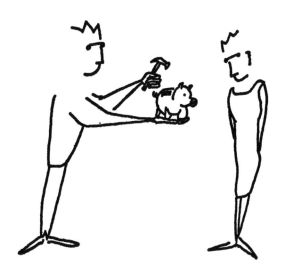

230. Make a time capsule together.

231. Go rollerblading together.

232. Buy your sweetheart a radar detector.

233. Share a blanket.

234. Surprise your sweetheart with a preplanned vacation for the two of you.

235. Leave a note in your sweetheart's business papers or on the bedpost.

236. Go out dancing together.

237. Go to a parade.

238. Plant a tree together.

239. Buy your sweetheart music that was popular when the two of you met.

240. Make your sweetheart this special dessert: a big brownie topped with a scoop of ice cream and hot fudge.

241. Clean the garage together.

242. Go to a toy store together.

243. Play an April Fool's joke on your sweetheart.

244. Decorate the Christmas tree together.

245. Go camping together.

246. Use a sauna together.

247. Go Christmas caroling together.

248. Have a gift shipped to your sweetheart.

249. Feed ducks together.

250. Start a hobby together.

251. Adopt a pet together.

252. Rake leaves together.

253. Look at old photos together.

254. Give your sweetheart some lingerie.

255. Buy your sweetheart a watch.

256. Have a return address stamper
made with both your names on it.

257. Play cards together.

258. Surprise your sweetheart with a gift in the middle of dinner.

259. Have a song you and your sweetheart can call "our song."

260. Run through sprinklers together.

261. Watch Saturday morning cartoons together.

262. Hold a door open for your sweetheart.

263. Carry your sweetheart's books or bags.

264. Have a baby.

265. Clip coupons together.

266. Enter a contest together.

267. Get a professional massage together.

268. Share an umbrella with your sweetheart.

269. Go back to the place(s) where you had your first date.

270. Use your sweetheart's name in a song as you sing it.

271. Make up a wedding guest list together.

272. Vote together.

273. Tickle your sweetheart.

274. Draw a bath for your sweetheart.

275. Ride a tandem bicycle together.

276. Use both of your voices on your answering machine greeting.

277. Get the oil changed in your sweetheart's car.

278. Compliment a part of your sweetheart's body. (hair

279. Shop for a car together.

280. Knit your sweetheart a sweater.

281. Buy your sweetheart a box of chocolates.

282. Take surfing lessons together.

283. Bake your sweetheart some cookies.

284. Set up a joint checking account.

285. Write "I love you" in the sand to your sweetheart.

286. Go sailing together.

287. Read the newspaper together.

288. Recycle together.

289. Squeeze a glass of fresh orange juice for your sweetheart.

290. Make your sweetheart the beneficiary of your life insurance policy.

291. Dance together at home.

292. Don't wake up your snoring sweetheart. Find somewhere else to sleep that night.

293. Give blood together.

294. Make pancakes with fruit in them for your sweetheart.

295. Climb a tree together.

296. Make snow angels together.

297. Watch free movies at a local college together.

298. Pick out your sweetheart's eyeglasses together.

299. Make popcorn for the two of you.

300. Play croquet.

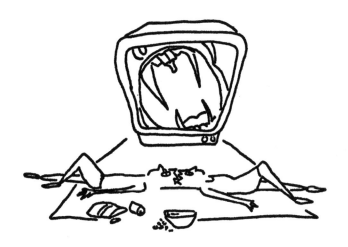

301. Watch TV all night together.

302. Keep a journal of your relationship.

303. Make hand- and footprints in wet cement together.

304. Buy your sweetheart some flavored coffees.

305. Listen to old albums, tapes, and compact discs together.

306. Order room service for your sweetheart.

307. Bring a cold drink when your
sweetheart is mowing the lawn.

for after practice

308. Play bingo together.

309. Have a photo taken of yourself for your sweetheart.

310. Go waterskiing together.

311. Buy your sweetheart a musical card.

312. Surprise your sweetheart with new carpeting. Have it put in while he is at work.

313. Rent out an RV for a road trip.

314. Wash the dog together.

315. When your sweetheart is sick, wait on her hand and foot.

316. Go swimming together.

317. Fluff up her pillow.

318. Buy your sweetheart some instant lottery tickets.

319. Make something out of wood for your sweetheart.

320. Pick your kids up after school together.

321. Whistle at your sweetheart.

322. Do a crossword puzzle together.

323. Go to the circus together.

324. Don't tell your sweetheart he has bad breath. Just offer him a piece of gum.

325. Take swimming lessons together.

326. Replace your sweetheart's old sneakers with brand-new ones.

327. Use the swings at a park together.

328. Take your sweetheart with you to conventions.

329. Put a message for your
sweetheart on a billboard.

A LOAF of BREAD AND A gallon of MILK.

330. Go to a museum together.

331. Rent out water vehicles.

332. Buy your sweetheart a car phone.

333. Pick out a painting for the house together.

334. Get a physical on the same day.

335. Wrestle with your sweetheart.

336. Plan out your kid's birthday party together.

337. Play pool with your sweetheart.

338. Hide Easter baskets for each other.

339. Take a train ride together.

340. Buy your sweetheart a set of china.

341. Clean out the attic together.

342. Bring your sweetheart Chinese takeout.

343. Take a bungee jump together.

344. Light candles with your sweetheart.

help sweeth with a
chore mowing lawn
raking leaves
cleaning out garage

345. Tag along when your sweetheart goes to a doctor appointment.

346. Buy your sweetheart some scented soaps.

347. Administer a home pregnancy
test together.

348. Skip stones on the water together.

349. Steal a kiss from your sweetheart.

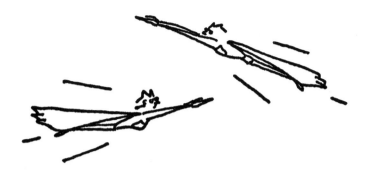

350. Tell your sweetheart that he is your hero.

351. Play raquetball together.

352. Type in a message for your sweetheart on his computer.

353. Build a gazebo together.

354. Watch a drag race together.

355. Send your sweetheart a telegram while you're out of town.

356. Get blue and pink toothbrushes for the two of you.

357. Sing in a choir together.

358. Watch a court case together.

359. Find things to give to charity together.

360. Get something repaired for your sweetheart.

361. Go to Lamaze classes together.

362. Go canoeing together.

363. Look at cloud formations together.

364. Shop for baby clothes together.

365. Tell your sweetheart that she is welcome to open your mail.

366. Start a greenhouse together.

367. Take an aerobics class together.

368. Go grocery shopping together.

369. Buy your sweetheart a music box.

370. Drive to work together.

371. Make your sweetheart a collage with pictures of the two of you.

372. When traveling abroad, buy your sweetheart a Cuban cigar.

373. Buy your sweetheart a subscription to a favorite publication.

374. Go out for breakfast together.

375. Dedicate a song on the radio to your sweetheart.

376. Have a personalized welcome mat made with both your names on it.

377. Do the dishes together.

378. Rent a hotel room together.

379. Build a sand castle together.

380. Buy your sweetheart jewelry with her birthstone.

381. Go out for lunch together.

382. Bite your sweetheart's ear.

383. Play a slot machine together.

384. Do your taxes together.

385. Have an ultrasound done of your unborn baby.

386. Rearrange the furniture together.

387. Buy your sweetheart a toolbox.

388. Go to an auction together.

389. Shop for a home together.

390. Buy your sweetheart an imported bottle of wine.

391. Make beer or wine together.

392. Watch an air show together.

393. Reserve your old honeymoon suite for your anniversary.

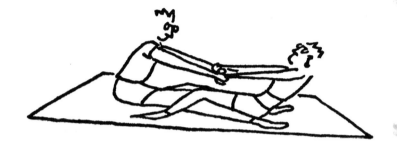

394. Exercise together.

395. Make caramel apples together.

396. Jump on a trampoline together.

397. Read your horoscopes together.

398. Learn first aid together.

halloween andy together

399. Wash your sweetheart's car.

400. Sing karaoke together.

401. Share a soft drink.

402. Try to get a job that allows you and your sweetheart to work together.

403. Get personalized champagne glasses for you and your sweetheart.

404. Buy a treadmill for the two of you.

405. Go to the Olympics together.

406. Pay your sweetheart's credit card bill.

407. Buy your sweetheart a tie.

408. Take part in a festival together.

409. Go ice skating together.

410. Ride a ferris wheel together.

411. Make sure you get the first slow
dance with your sweetheart.

412. Thank your sweetheart for something.

413. Make s'mores with your sweetheart.

414. Make your sweetheart the sole heir of your will.

415. Buy your sweetheart a membership in a fan club.

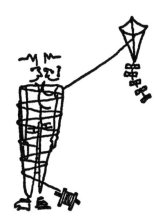

416. Fly a kite together.

417. Pick some wildflowers for your sweetheart.

418. Shave your sweetheart's legs.

419. Ride a waterslide together.

420. Adopt a child together.

421. Shop for bathing suits together.

422. In addition to giving your sweetheart a birthday gift, give his mother a gift in appreciation for giving birth to him.

423. Go to Mardi Gras together.

424. Walk the dog together.

425. Have your work or school schedules coincide as much as possible.

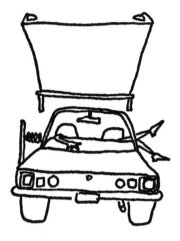

426. Go to a drive-in movie together.

427. Buy your sweetheart a beer stein.

428. Buy him a moustache-grooming set.

429. Shovel snow together.

430. Take a boat ride together.

431. Give out Halloween candy together.

432. Buy your sweetheart personalized golf balls.

433. Paint your sweetheart's nails.

434. Have a garage sale together.

435. Learn a second language together.

436. Replace the windshield wipers on your sweetheart's car with winter wipers.

437. Play fetch with the dog.

438. Give your sweetheart your frequent flyer miles.

439. Before your sweetheart goes shopping, give him some money to buy something nice.

440. Tell your sweetheart that he has nice legs.

441. Take a bath together.

442. Buy your sweetheart a big plant.

443. Do yard work together.

444. Have a pillow fight with your sweetheart.

445. Decorate your sweetheart's office on a special day.

446. When you sign up for a video rental membership, sign up your sweetheart as well.

447. Make a milkshake for your sweetheart.

448. Buy your sweetheart a proof set of coins from the year you married.

449. Have something for dinner that you and your sweetheart haven't had in a long time.

450. Play together on a teeter-totter.

451. Personalize the mailbox with your names.

452. Make your sweetheart a glass of chocolate milk.

453. Play shuffleboard together.

454. Decorate Easter eggs together.

455. Let your sweetheart win an argument.

456. Play darts together.

457. Keep your sweetheart's medical information in your wallet.

458. Rub suntan lotion on each other.

459. Play catch together.

460. Write your sweetheart a message on the toilet paper roll.

461. Have a snowball fight.

462. Instead of dropping your sweetheart off at the airport, stay until she boards the plane.

463. Consider writing your own wedding vows.

464. Play with your sweetheart's hair.

465. Play miniature golf together.

466. Watch the news together.

467. Hold on to your sweetheart when you walk across ice.

468. Make a point each day to give some of your extra time to your sweetheart.

469. Have new tires put on your sweetheart's car.

470. Have your hair dyed together.

471. Do stretches together.

472. Give your sweetheart a haircut

473. Buy your sweetheart an easy chair.

474. Volunteer to be Santa and Mrs. Claus for children.

475. Get your sweetheart something from the kitchen during commercials.

476. Buy your sweetheart some allergy medicine.

477. Go rollerskating together.

478. Catch fireflies together.

479. When your sweetheart is tired, volunteer to change the baby's diaper.

480. Buy your sweetheart his favorite music video.

481. Visit historic sites together.

482. Get your fortune told together.

483. Wink at your sweetheart.

484. Play a musical instrument for your sweetheart.

485. When your sweetheart has a cold, buy extra soft tissues that have lotion in them.

486. Start a daily regimen of taking vitamins.

487. Buy a toy or treat for your sweetheart's pet.

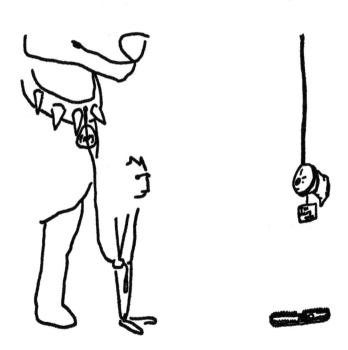

488. Buy bean bags for the two of you.

489. Remodel your kitchen together.

490. Buy your sweetheart a sports cap of his favorite team.

491. Share a stick of gum with your sweetheart.

492. Do a jigsaw puzzle together.

493. Make one of your sweetheart's dreams come true.

494. Make hot chocolate for your sweetheart.

495. Let your sweetheart hog the bed.

496. Take dance lessons together.

497. Make sure your sweetheart's bags are packed when she is very pregnant.

498. Let your sweetheart think she is "the boss."

499. Get "his" and "hers" towels.

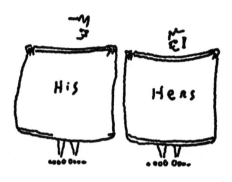

500. Give your sweetheart a big hug.

Bonus: Since I'm such a sweetheart, I'll give you an extra idea—buy your sweetheart this book.